Materials

Soil

Chris Oxlade

Heinemann

www.heinemann.co.uk/library
Visit our website to find out more information about **Heinemann Library** books.

To Order:
☎ Phone 44 (0) 1865 888066
🖹 Send a fax to 44 (0) 1865 314091
💻 Visit the Heinemann Library Bookshop at www.heinemann.co.uk/library to browse our catalogue and order online.

First published in Great Britain by Heinemann Library, Halley Court, Jordan Hill, Oxford OX2 8EJ a division of Reed Educational and Professional Publishing Ltd.
Heinemann is a registered trademark of Reed Educational & Professional Publishing Ltd.

OXFORD MELBOURNE AUCKLAND JOHANNESBURG BLANTYRE
GABORONE IBADAN PORTSMOUTH (NH) USA CHICAGO

Designed by Storeybooks
Originated by Ambassador Litho Ltd.
Printed and bound in Hong Kong/China

ISBN 0 431 12735 2 (hardback)   ISBN 0 431 12741 7 (paperback)
06 05 04 03 02   06 05 04 03 02
10 9 8 7 6 5 4 3 2   10 9 8 7 6 5 4 3 2 1

British Library Cataloguing in Publication Data
Oxlade, Chris
Soil. – (Materials)
1.Soils – Juvenile literature
I.Title
631.4

Acknowledgements
The Publishers would like to thank the following for permission to reproduce photographs:
Chapel Studios: Zul Mukhida p11; Corbis: p10; Ecoscene: p25, Andrew Brown pp9, 15, Chinch Gryniewicz p5, Sally Morgan p4, Tony Page p23; FLPA: p8; GSF Picture Library: pp12, 14, 18, 26; Hodder Wayland: p24; Impact: Piers Cavendish p20; NHPA: Eric Soder p29; Oxford Scientific Films: p27, Irvine Cushing p21, David M Dennis p16; Science Photo Library: p17; Still Pictures: pp13, 22; Tudor Photography: pp6, 7, 19.

Cover photograph reproduced with permission of Image Bank.

Every effort has been made to contact copyright holders of any material reproduced in this book. Any omissions will be rectified in subsequent printings if notice is given to the Publisher.

Contents

What is soil? 4

What's in soil? 6

Soil colours 8

Soil and water 10

Rocks in the soil 12

Humus 14

Animals in the soil 16

Growing in soil 18

Growing crops 20

Keeping soil fresh 22

Building with soil 24

Spoiling soil 26

Fact file 28

Would you believe it? 29

Glossary 30

More books to read 32

Index 32

You can find words shown in bold, **like this,** in the Glossary.

What is soil?

Soil is a **natural** material. You find soil where plants grow. Soil covers the top part of the ground in gardens, fields and woodlands.

Plants, from tiny flowers to huge trees, cannot live without soil. Soil contains the **nutrients** and water that plants need to grow.

What's in soil?

Soil is made up of different materials.
One material is rock, broken into bits.
Some bits of rock are large pebbles.
Some are tiny grains, too small to see.

Soil contains bits of dead plants, such as leaves and twigs. They slowly **rot** away. These bits are called **humus**. Many tiny animals also live in soil.

Soil colours

There are many different types of soil.
This soil contains tiny grains of rock
that make it a browny-red colour. It is
called clay soil.

This soil is very dark brown. It contains lots of **rotting** roots and leaves, and grains of sand. It is called peat. It is found in wet, **boggy** places.

Soil and water

There are spaces between the bits of rock and **humus** in the soil. There are large spaces between the grains of sand in sandy soil. Rainwater quickly **drains** through them.

The bits of rock in clay soil are very tiny. There are only small spaces between the bits. Rainwater cannot drain quickly through them. It lies on top of the clay in puddles.

Rocks in the soil

The bits of rock in soil come from
rocks and mountains. Rocks are
broken up by wind and by water.
They are also heated up by the Sun,
which makes them crack.

When rain falls on the ground, it washes the bits of rock into streams and rivers. If the river **floods**, the rocky soil is left on the land next to the river.

Humus

Humus is the name for the bits of dead plants in the soil. Humus is made of leaves that fall from trees, and from the roots, stems and leaves of dead plants.

Very slowly the leaves and dead plants **rot** away. They turn brown and mushy. In the end, they become part of the soil. Humus helps to stop the soil drying up.

Animals in the soil

Many different animals live in the soil. Worms **burrow** through the soil. As they burrow, they break the soil up. This lets air and water into the soil and helps plants to grow.

There are millions of tiny living things in the soil. They eat dead bits of plants and animals, turning them into **humus**. You can only see some of them through a **microscope**.

Growing in soil

As a plant grows, its roots grow down
into the soil. Roots grip the soil and
stop plants toppling over in the
wind. Tall trees have huge roots
deep underground.

A plant's roots collect water and **nutrients** from the soil. The plant needs these to live and grow. Tiny root hairs stick out from the root. They collect the water and nutrients.

Growing Crops

Farmers grow their **crops** in fields of soil. Before they plant seeds, they prepare the soil. They dig it over with a **plough**. This brings fresh soil to the top.

Gardeners also prepare soil before they grow plants. They dig the soil with a spade. This brings fresh soil to the top and breaks the soil into small pieces.

Keeping soil fresh

Plants take **nutrients** from the soil.
When the plants die, they **rot** away. This
puts the nutrients back into the soil.
Gardeners add rotted plants to the soil
to keep it healthy.

Farmers gather the **crops** in their fields. This means there are no plants left to put nutrients into the soil. The farmer has to add **fertilizer** to put the nutrients back.

Building with soil

Soil can be used to build strong walls
called banks. Banks hold back the
water when a river rises after heavy
rain. Sometimes the river washes the
banks away and **floods** the land.

Farmers grow rice in flooded fields called paddy fields. Rice needs a lot of water to grow. The farmers build banks of soil around the fields to keep the water in.

Spoiling soil

Soil is easily broken up. If too many trees are cut down, there are no tree roots to keep the soil together. Heavy rain washes the soil away.

Soil can be spoiled by **pollution**. Bits of
rubbish and **chemicals** spilled on the soil
make it hard for plants to grow there.
Only some tough weeds can survive.

Fact file

- Soil is a **natural** material.

- Soils come in many different colours.

- All soils have tiny bits of rock in them.

- Some soils have large bits of rock in them.

- Some soils let water **drain** away easily.

- Some soils stop water draining away.

- Soil contains **nutrients** that plants need to live and grow.

- Soil does not burn when it is heated.

- Soil does not let electricity flow through it.

- Soil is not attracted by magnets.

Would you believe it?

Earthworms eat soil as they **burrow** through it! They take the goodness out of the soil and pass the rest out again. A worm cast is a tiny heap of soil that a worm has eaten!

Glossary

boggy   ground that is very wet

burrow   to dig a hole in the ground. Animals that live underground burrow down into the soil.

chemicals   special materials that are used in factories and homes to do many jobs, including cleaning

crops   plants that farmers grow for food, such as wheat and potatoes

drain   to dry up because water flows away. Soil drains because water flows down through it.

fertilizer   chemicals full of nutrients that farmers put on their fields to help plants grow better

flood   when the water in a river flows over the river banks

humus   parts of soil that are made from bits of dead animals and plants

microscope   something that makes things look bigger than they are

natural   comes from plants, animals or the rocks in the Earth

nutrients   chemicals that plants need to live and grow

plough   machine that digs the soil in fields before crops are planted

pollution   rubbish or poisonous chemicals that are thrown on to the ground or into the air, rivers and seas

rot, rotting   be eaten away by tiny animals and plants in the ground

More books to read

Images: Materials and Their Properties
Big Book Compilation
Heinemann Library, 1999

My World of Science
Angela Royston
Heinemann Library, 2001

New Star Science: Materials and Their Uses
Ginn, 2001

New Star Science: Rocks and Soil
Ginn, 2001

See for Yourself: Soil
Karen Bryant-Mole
A&C Black, 1995

Index

animals   7, 16–17
clay   8, 11
colours of soil   8–9, 28
crops   20, 23
fertilizer   23
flooding   13, 24
humus   7, 14–15, 17
nutrients   5, 19, 22–23, 28
peat   9

pollution   27
rice   25
river banks   24
rock   6, 8, 10–11, 12–13, 28
roots   9, 14, 18–19, 26
sand   9, 10
water   5, 10–11, 12, 16, 19, 24, 25, 28
worms   16, 29